Byers' Choice Ltd.

The Carolers

A HANDCRAFTED
CHRISTMAS TRADITION

A Treasury of Carolers

Byers' Choice Ltd.

The Carolers
A HANDCRAFTED CHRISTMAS TRADITION

A Treasury of Carolers

JOYCE BYERS

FRIEDMAN/FAIRFAX
PUBLISHERS

A FRIEDMAN/FAIRFAX BOOK

©1998 by Michael Friedman Publishing Group, Inc.

Library of Congress Cataloging-in-Publication data available
upon request

ISBN 1-56799-690-6

Editor: Francine Hornberger
Designer: Andrea Karman
Photography Director: Christopher C. Bain
Principle photography by Bill Milne

Color separations by Colourscan Co. Pte. Ltd
Printed in Singapore by KHL Printing Co. Pte. Ltd.

1 3 5 7 9 10 8 6 4 2

For bulk purchases and special sales, please contact:
Friedman/Fairfax Publishers
Attention: Sales Department
15 West 26th Street
New York, New York 10010
212/685-6610   FAX 212/685-1307

Visit our website:
http://www.metrobooks.com

DEDICATION

We dedicate this book to all the people we've met along the way.
As Tiny Tim is known to say, "May God bless us, everyone."

ACKNOWLEDGMENTS

We wish to give special thanks to Francine Hornberger
for her kindness, sensitivity, and wisdom, and to Lisa Porter
for unselfishly giving her time and talents to sift through the many facts
and details incorporated into this book. Without their help
we would still be on page one.

Part Two

Our Favorite Carolers
from the Past Twenty Years

40

Dear Byers' Choice,

I have only been collecting Carolers for a year, and already I have fourteen of them. I love them so much that they are all I ask for—for my birthday, anniversary, Christmas, Mother's Day, etc. I am addicted! You should be so proud of your company. The quality and creativity of each piece is superb!

Well, I guess what I am trying to say to you, is there are people out there, like me, who absolutely adore and treasure these little creatures. They bring such joy to our lives. I love receiving your newsletters and especially loved the Christmas ornament I received this year. Thank you! Have a wonderful New Year and Good Luck to your fantastic company.

Warmest wishes,
Kathleen Franko
January 1993

Introduction

Joyce and Bob Byers have realized a dream. The Christmas Caroler figurines they create in their Bucks County workshop are widely collected throughout the United States and beyond. They are treasured not only as collectibles, but for the way they represent a simpler time and way of life; a belief in family and community and honest-to-goodness caring about people. The main premise of the Byers' Choice organization has always been to serve God and to "give something back," whether that something be a delightful figurine whose mouth is poised in praise to God, or in the form of donations made to charities large and small. All one need do is visit the charming workshop in Chalfont, Pennsylvania, to get a sense of what makes up Byers' Choice Ltd.®

Now, in their twentieth year of bringing Christmas joy and tradition to the world, the Byers present a wonderful collection of their favorite Christmas treasures. Inside this volume, you will learn all about Byers' Choice. Our history and our message are brought out in part one, as is a trip to our workshop where you'll meet the people who help make Byers' Choice magic. Part two showcases some of our favorite

A VICTORIAN FAMILY

SCHOOLTEACHER (1992–94) and SCHOOL KIDS (1993–94)

POSTMAN (1990–93)

Carolers from the past twenty years and features the stories that have gone into their making. Chapters include: Christmas Around the World; Santa Claus and Mrs. Claus; Charles Dickens' London; and Holiday Traditions and Christmas Joy Throughout the Year.

For collectors, for shops, for family, for friends, this *Treasury of Carolers* is a gift to you for all your love and support through the years. Enjoy your journey through the past twenty years of Caroler magic!

Dear Joyce & Bob,
Our sincere best wishes to you and your staff on your twentieth anniversary.
We also are celebrating being your customers for the past twenty years, and God willing, we can all continue as partners in this wonderful endeavor.

With much admiration,
Anne Marie &
Jim Radicioni

PART ONE

What Byers' Choice Is All About

"BECAUSE HE LOVES ME," SAYS THE LORD, "I WILL RESCUE HIM;

I WILL PROTECT HIM, FOR HE ACKNOWLEDGES MY NAME.

HE WILL CALL UPON ME, AND I WILL ANSWER HIM;

I WILL BE WITH HIM IN TROUBLE,

I WILL DELIVER HIM AND HONOR HIM.

WITH LONG LIFE WILL I SATISFY HIM

AND SHOW HIM MY SALVATION."

—PSALM 91: 14–16

Chapter One

The History, the Family, Our Driving Force

PUPPETEER (1996–)

Dear Bob & Joyce,
Thank you for the bridge that shelters us from the rain.
And helping the Salvation Army for those who have so
much to gain.
Thank you for your word of God at Christmas.
And your teaching of life's happenings that we might
be missing.
Thank you for your open ear to hear our troubles.
And generosity to all of us through all our rubble.
Thank you for the feelings you share.
And for all the time you spare.

Holly DeVoe

The original mold for each Caroler's face is hand-sculpted by Joyce; specially trained artisans add the finishing touches.

THE HISTORY

Although 1998 is the twentieth anniversary of Byers' Choice, the company really began in the mid 1960s, when figures were created at the Byers' own kitchen table. These early Carolers were intended as gifts and decorations for the homes of relatives and friends at Christmas. Joyce was inspired to make these figures, as she was worried about what Christmas had become in recent years. The commercialization of the holiday was starting to ruin the idea of Christmas that Joyce had always known, and she wanted desperately to bring back the feeling of an old-fashioned Christmas.

"My Christmas had never involved a lot of flash and sparkle. Tin foil trees weren't my idea of a symbol of the season, and I started to feel a deep loss of tradition.... One of my favorite parts of any Christmas celebration was singing carols, and I thought, why not design carolers to use as Christmas decorations?"

Joyce Remembers

When I was a child, the highlight of Christmas Day was gathering with the family at my grandparents' farm. Four generations would join under one roof to exchange gifts and share food. Although the gifts were rather modest—every year my grandmother gave each of the men a pair of black socks—the food was extraordinary.

The meal began with fruit cocktail made from fruits from the farm, either canned or stored in the root cellar. Delicious bread was baked by my Aunt Ann. Three meats were served: turkey, ham, and game. There would be sweet and mashed potatoes and several vegetables. Succotash would always be served. Since my grandparents were Pennsylvania Dutch, seven sweets and seven sours were also on the table. These sweets and sours included things like chow-chow, red beet eggs, and pickled watermelon rind. Of course, there was always dessert—homemade ice cream and assorted cakes and pies. The Christmas cookies were a subject unto themselves. A Christmas hostess fell short unless she presented a tray with at least a dozen different types of Christmas cookies. Each family had its favorites, but the variety was essential. This feast was prepared on a wood burning cook stove, leaving the modern gas range sitting quietly by.

I loved my grandmother's Christmas tree because it twinkled with hand-blown glass balls and animals, lights with bubbles, and ornaments made by my mother and her sisters years before.

An amateur artist with a degree in fashion design from Drexel University in Philadelphia, Joyce had the background to prepare her for her figurine-making venture. Using materials she found around her house and tapping into her fertile imagination, she created the first versions of the Byers' Choice Christmas Carolers.

"A bent wire for an armature, newspaper to pad out the body, and clay to sculpt a head, and I was on my way!" remembers Joyce. "Scraps of fabric, leather, and fur combined to form our 1965 Christmas decorations. Everyone seemed to enjoy them, so of course in 1966, caroling figures became the gift for family and friends. One friend, who visited while these gifts were being made, suggested that I try selling them at a nearby woman's exchange. I did, and to my surprise they sold. This kept us up Christmas Eve finishing the gifts to be given Christmas morning.

"The Wayne Woman's Exchange in Wayne, Pennsylvania, encouraged other woman's exchanges to carry my caroling figures. Over a ten-year period this developed into a seasonal hobby, which was at times pleasurable and at times quite hectic. More than once I begged a crafty friend to take it off my hands." Luckily for us all, Joyce continued.

Dear Byers' Choice,

I am writing this letter on behalf of my sister, Angie, and myself. We are both avid collectors of Byers' Choice figurines, which we have been collecting since the 1980s. We were very, very lucky this year, because our sister Julie generously gave us a Caroler with a male cardinal on his arm, which represents a special reminder of our departed mother. I cherish the love and generosity with which it was given.

Best wishes for a happy and prosperous New Year.

Sincerely,
Lisa A. Fischer
North Attleboro, MA

Bob also attended Drexel, where he earned a business degree—and where he and Joyce met. The two were married on Christmas Eve, 1963, in Joyce's hometown of Quarryville, Pennsylvania. Their two sons, Robert Jr. and Jeff, were born in 1965 and 1967, respectively.

In the mid 1970s, Bob and Joyce started two businesses. One was restoring old houses; the second was selling antiques. But a dip in the real estate market caused them to realize the housing industry might not provide the security they were looking for. The antiques business, which they named Byers' Choice, was really just a hobby at that time, but during the Christmas season, they included Joyce's caroling figures along with the antiques. As fate would have it, they sold far more Carolers than antiques.

Seeing the demand for the figures, Bob took a dozen to the New York Gift Show in 1978, hoping to find someone to represent their product. There was a lot of excitement about the Carolers at the show—and the rest is history. The Byers' Choice anniversary is counted from this year, when the Carolers were first sold nationally. On May 29, 1981, several full-time workers were added to the staff of Caroler makers, and the family incorporated its business as Byers' Choice Ltd.

Byers' Choice is still a family business. Joyce creates the prototype for each Caroler, sculpting all the face molds and designing the clothing; Bob handles the financial and administrative side of the business and oversees The Byers Foundation, which gives extensively to many local, national, and international charitable concerns; Bob Jr. oversees each figurine through production; and Jeff joined the company in 1990 as creative assistant to Joyce and marketing manager. Bob Jr.'s wife, Pam, and Jeff's wife, Dawn, are very busy raising small children, but they have both been very supportive and continue to help with projects such as the *Caroler Chronicle* newsletter.

First figurines, circa 1965.

IT ISN'T ABOUT MONEY

As Byers' Choice Ltd. has grown throughout the years, so, too, has the company's philosophy toward serving God, its customers, the wider community which encompasses it, and its employees. With realization of the great blessings which have been bestowed on himself and his family, Bob Byers has refined his personal beliefs, which are at the core of the guiding precepts of his company. A strong sense of responsibility has shaped Bob's attitude and has molded the company's philosophies into what they are today.

"We're just stewards of God's blessings," he says. Those who have been blessed abundantly need to loosen up...give more...and enjoy a life of real significance! Unfortunately, a lot of monetarily successful people seem to give little thought as to how the Lord would like them to use their blessings."

Joyce agrees that monetary concerns—beyond the successful running of the business—aren't their driving force. "We aren't people who need or want a lot of material things. We live very comfortably and have a lot of extra. We're just glad to share that with as many people as we can."

Since making money is "not number one on the list" for the Byers, Bob established The Byers Foundation in 1986. It is the philanthropic arm of the corporation, which helps donate over twenty percent of the company's profits to charities and nonprofit cultural organizations. Last year the family, the company, and the Foundation gave meaningful assistance to hundreds of charitable organizations.

Dear Mr. & Mrs. Byers,

Because of persons such as you, sharing with others the blessings that God has bestowed upon you, this world is a much better place. We are encouraged and grateful for your generous gift to our church.

As members of the Bright Hope Baptist Church family, we try to provide a spiritual haven for those in need. As a choir, we strive to inspire all who hear us, by lifting up the Lord in song. We are delighted that you enjoyed the Habitat for Humanity Concert as much as we enjoyed being a part of it. Mr. Dumpson informed me of your interest in helping Celestial Choir in the production of our first CD recording.

Sincerely,
Charles E. West, President
Celestial Choir

Some of the benefactors of the Byers' largesse include the Salvation Army (see pages 24–25), Covenant House, Young Life, YMCA, area hospitals and free clinics, art museums, Christ's Home, local churches and shelters, and MAP, an organization through which they have helped ship millions of dollars worth of medicines to third world countries.

One of their local projects, Business Cares, which was started by the Byers in the late 1980s, is now an annual event sponsored through the Central Bucks Chamber of Commerce. The project encourages chamber members to donate to Business Cares, which distributes the funds to improve the lives of the needy, especially during the holidays. Agencies involved include Meals on Wheels, Dental Care for the Needy, the Doylestown Free Clinic, FISH, and Tabor Children's Services.

Another community improvement effort started by Bob and Joyce is Bucks Beautiful, a dynamic effort to encourage the planting of public and commercial gardens. Subscribers receive a limited edition Caroler (different every year), and the money collected is distributed in grants of up to $2,000 for anyone who wants to plant a community garden. Each year there is a friendly competition among the participants to see who can create the most beautiful and creative landscaping. Over $100,000 in grants have been awarded, but the major fund provider is still Byers' Choice Ltd. The Byers believe the desire for community beautification through flowers should come naturally, and they know that it adds so much to the quality of life. Over one hundred new community gardens now welcome visitors to Bucks County as a result of this program.

Through an employee giving campaign, which includes the preparation of over two hundred Thanksgiving dinners for the needy, the Byers have instilled their belief that giving of one's money, time, and talent are God-given responsibilities of us all, and their work has set an example to businesses and individuals

The entrance to the Byers' Choice headquarters in Chalfont, Pennsylvania.

Dear Bob:

We would like to take this opportunity on Valentine's Day to thank you "from the bottom of our heart" for supporting us in our efforts to serve the community.

Because you cared so much, and gave so much more, our association was able to impact thousands of lives last year: over $60,000 in financial assistance was distributed to area children and families; more than 3,800 children attended summer day camp so their parents could work; more than 1,700 children had a safe place to go before and after school; and 34,000 children participated in youth development programs such as Black Achievers, teen nights, basketball, gymnastics, and roller and street hockey. It's also important for you to know that all YMCA programs continue to emphasize the Character Development values of caring, honesty, respect and responsibility.

On behalf of the YMCA of Philadelphia and vicinity, please accept the "heartfelt" thank you enclosed--it was created especially for you by one of the kids in our child care program. Let it serve as a reminder to you of the lives you have touched through your kindness and generosity.

D. Allan Shaffer
President
YMCA of Philadelphia Vicinity

across the region. Bob and Joyce Byers and their two sons have created a mid-size company with community roots that extend internationally. Just as their Christmas Carolers are lovingly hand-molded by individual crafters, the Byers have hand-crafted their giving strategy to include giving to religious organizations, youth programs, medical causes, and the arts.

The Byers' philosophy: it is truly by giving that one receives and by a positive example that one teaches.

Dear Mr. Beyers:

RE: Donation - Flood Relief

Thanks so much for your continuing strong support of our Salvation Army. The National Commander has told me of your recent support of The Salvation Army's work in the Mid-West Floods and several other projects. It is tremendously encouraging to have friends like you support the Army.

Your support for the William Booth Society and re-building our facilities in Pakistan shows that your interest goes far beyond the Army in your local setting. It is great to have you on our National Board, Bob.

May God bless you.

Sincerely,
Major Tom Jones
National Community Relations
& Development Secretary.

Salvation Army characters from left: MAN WITH CORNET (1993–1997); BOY WITH FLAG (1997–); WOMAN WITH RED KETTLE (1992–); WOMAN WITH TAMBOURINE (1994–95); MAN WITH BASS DRUM (1996–); GIRL WITH WAR CRY (1995–); MAN WITH TUBA (1998–)

The Salvation Army

The charity closest to the Byers' hearts is the Salvation Army, for which a collection bucket stands proudly in the lobby of their showplace. A portion of the proceeds from the sale of each of the Caroler figurines in the Salvation Army line goes to this organization that provides help to so many needy people.

In 1992, the Salvation Army gave Byers' Choice permission to design a line of figures representing Salvation Army members. Joyce introduced the line with the Salvation Army Woman with Kettle in 1992, the one hundredth anniversary of the Salvation Army's trademark red kettle symbol. Since then, Joyce has created about half a dozen more in the series. Licensing fees and additional contributions from the Byers go to support the work of the Salvation Army as it ministers to the physical and spiritual needs of anyone requiring its help. And the Byers hope these figurines will inspire others to join in the Army's spirit of caring and sharing.

The Salvation Army Boy with Flag is one of the youngest members of the organization. He proudly carries the flag that bears the three primary colors of the Salvation Army, each representing a part of the Trinity. The blue border stands for God's holiness; the red field symbolizes the blood of Jesus; and the eight-pointed yellow star, with the inscription "Blood and Fire," represents the power of the Holy Spirit.

No Salvation Army scene would be complete without the Salvation Army Band. A female Caroler, dressed in the distinctive blue and red of the Army, calls attention to her cause with a tambourine, while her male companions, dressed in matching colors, play a cornet, a drum, and a tuba. The group represents the true spirit of Christmas—giving.

In 1995, Bob and Joyce were invited to attend the Salvation Army School for Officer Training graduation, where they were named the first two Samuel Logan Brengle Fellows. At the ceremony, they were cited for their service to the Army as volunteers for their annual giving, Christian witness, and the establishment of two full perpetuating cadet scholarships for the School for Officer Training in the Eastern U.S. Territory.

"We have been incredibly impressed by the Salvation Army's dedication to its work of serving Christ and helping mankind," said Bob. "It has had a profound impact on the way Joyce and I have chosen to run our business."

The Order of Samuel Logan Brengle Fellows is named for a man who dedicated his life to the work of the Salvation Army. In the early 1900s, Brengle rose through the ranks of the Army to become a spiritual mentor to Salvation Army leaders around the world. This fellowship was established "to honor those who make significant contributions to the enhancement of the training of officers in the Eastern U.S. Territory."

Chapter Two

The Workshop

and the Artisans...

TRADITIONAL BOY

Dear Mr. & Mrs. Byers,
This note of thanks is long overdue and you probably don't hear it enough. For all the wonderful things you do for all of us employees here at Byers' Choice, you've made it a pleasant place to work and I'm very happy here. Thank you again!

An Employee

THE COMPANY IS THE FAMILY

"I believe we have a responsibility toward four things: God, our customers, our employees, and the community," says Bob Byers, who lives out that responsibility daily in many ways, both large and small. "One of the things we have done to fulfill that responsibility is to make our workshop a showplace, an attractive place to come and one which adds to the value of Byers' Choice, and helps increase area tourism—and helps us to be an asset to the community. We want our visitors to have fun coming here, and we want our employees to have fun here, too. Work shouldn't be drudgery."

The bright and airy work area at Byers' Choice is complete with individual headsets for employees to listen to audiotapes of music or books, but this is just part of the overall workplace. The employee parking lot is situated behind a veil of trees in back of the large corporate headquarters, whose twenty-six acres include carefully landscaped lawns dotted with realistic bronze sculptures of children at play. A covered walkway, lined with hanging floral baskets in summertime, leads from the parking lot to the main building and passes through a rest area complete with picnic tables. The cafeteria is tastefully decorated, and in the fall and winter fresh cut flowers adorn each table. One wall is a gallery, named "The Great Wall of Byers' Choice," of photographs of all the employees. When Bob is asked about this, he jokingly replies, "China has a Great Wall, but I decided to make a better one!"

The company has a premiere art collection, most of which was painted by artists from the Pennsylvania Impressionist School. The paintings are exhibited on the walls throughout the entire complex. A first-name policy is in effect, which encourages the feeling that co-workers are not just acquaintances, but rather, are more

(continued on page 31)

Early figurines, circa late 1960s.

A TRADITIONAL FAMILY

like family. The overall feeling at Byer's Choice is one that is warm and friendly; the staff is treated with dignity and respect.

"It's not something we work at," says Patty O'Donnell, who is the manager of the Gift Emporium. "It's all because of Bob and Joyce, and the way they run the business and treat the people here like we're all part of a team, like a family. Besides, we work in Santa's workshop— how could we not like it?"

Bob stresses that accessibility to staff is an all-important part of his business administration, and part of his belief in levels of responsibility. "We should be there for them in any emergency; they're part of our extended family," he says. "After all, if we don't care about them, why should they care about us?"

Dear Bob & Joyce,

This is my last year at Parsons—I love it! I know that I wouldn't be here if it wasn't for you!! Thank you!! I am going to graduate in May and would love to use my Interior Design background to make movie sets. I'll keep you posted. Have a wonderful holiday and thank you for all that you have done for my mother and me.

Sincerely,
Rebecca

Dear Bob & Joyce,

You've been on my mind lately so I thought I'd drop you a note to say hello. The other day Bonnie (who is now in kindergarten!) said to me, "When I grow up and get a job I'm going to work at Byers' Choice." I asked her why and she said, "Because it's the only fun place to work!" Do you think you'll have an opening in 10–15 years?

Love,
Sandy Brown

Byers' Choice Ltd. practices toward its employees just what it preaches through its profit-sharing plan (a pension plan into which the company has never put less than ten percent of an employee's salary per year); a very generous Christmas bonus; a scholarship program for employees' children; and other non-financial, but just as important perks—the week off between Christmas and New Years and an annual Halloween party where everyone dresses up in elaborate costumes and prizes are awarded.

Indeed, feelings run high among staff, sales reps, retailers, and customers alike for the Byers family. The example they set of the ability to run an extremely successful business while at the same time maintaining and encouraging loyalty and even love among those they come in contact with is, or should be, an example to other businesspeople everywhere.

Bob and Joyce have lived up to their ideal to create a showplace for their customers with first-class products and service, through their sense of responsibility to their employees and through evangelism to other businesspeople. Bob actively encourages others to fund charitable concerns and treats his employees with only the utmost respect and caring.

Dear Mr. Byers,

There are no words to express my gratitude. I am overwhelmed by your kindness and generosity. I have never in my life met anyone like you. I was at the end of my rope. I was praying to God for an answer, and there you were again answering my prayers.

I thank the Lord and you for helping me at my darkest hour. I hope I will always continue to be a loyal employee at your company. My boys and I thank you again.

God bless you.
Teresa Aimone

HOW ARE THE CAROLERS MADE?

When asked, "What was the best part of your visit to Byers' Choice?" a visitor almost always replies, "The observation deck. It is fascinating to watch the figures being made."

Tucked off in a corner of the production area is the plaster room. Here, a team of workers takes armatures made from bent wires and gently places them into soft plaster. "It's kind of like making cookies," says one woman, as she spoons the exact amount of plaster necessary to make a base onto a work surface. "Plaster sets up fast, and we really have to keep moving."

When the plaster has dried, the base is painted a dark green, for which Byers' Choice figures are noted. Next, the armature goes to a crafter, who will sculpt a body with paper. Each body varies slightly depending on how the sculptor handles the paper. Interestingly, thin people tend to sculpt thin bodies and heavier people sculpt more robust shapes.

While the bodies are being made, another group of artists makes the heads. Joyce sculpts the original face and creates a master mold. To capture the initial expression of each character takes only minutes. The process of preparing a good, workable mold, however, can take days. Joyce is an incorrigible people watcher. But she doesn't try to copy a particular face. She captures the character and expressions *behind* the face. This somewhat impressionistic interpretation is what admirers of the Carolers enjoy most.

An artist takes a chunk of clay, presses it into a mold, removes it, applies undercuts, and smoothes the surface. Because the clay is very soft at this stage, the slightest amount of pressure will change the shape of the face. Some faces will become elongated, some noses will be turned up, and some chins will be turned down. Each artist uses her own technique to bring the face to life.

The next step is to apply a coat of flesh-colored paint. To get it smooth is trickier than you may think. Then the head is ready for features. An artist painting eyes remarked, "I love this job. I can paint the eyes whatever color I feel like mixing today. I can paint rosy cheeks on children

The painting of the Carolers' faces.

Early figurine, circa 1966.

An artisan carefully sculpts the body of a Caroler.

and sad eyes on old men. Each one speaks to me." The supervisor keeps a close eye on each head to make sure this freedom of judgment is kept within bounds. She recalls one feature painter—who was having a really bad day— painting frowning eyebrows on every face. The following day she had to repaint all of them!

The cutting and sewing department is about as high-tech as Byers' Choice gets. Here thousands of small pieces of clothing are made. Because the pieces are so small, accuracy is very important. A miscalculation of one half inch is equivalent to a three-inch mistake in a regular size garment. The miniature garments require skill and patience on the part of those who sew them. Nimble fingers in this department will tie tens of thousands of bows in just one year.

The dressing area where all the parts arrive for final assembly is the area most visible to visitors. The clothing is actually simulated. The sleeves, for example, are not sewn into the jacket. The craftsman who does the final assembly receives two cylindrical pieces of fabric for sleeves, a rectangular collar, and one of many shapes used for a jacket. She must drape these parts onto the body, and with the use of glue and pins, shape the pieces to simulate a jacket.

One dresser said, "This is fun. It is constantly changing because we only make one hundred of any one design. We are encouraged to put lots of personality into each figure. It's amazing to see the number of versions you can get with a few scraps of fabric, trims, a little bit of fur, and a bend of the head or the positioning of an arm."

Visitors frequently comment, "The people who dress the Carolers move so quickly." This is true, but behind the scenes, it sometimes takes years for a craftsman to be trained to be able to achieve the look and quality Byers' Choice is known for within a time frame that enables the figures to be made in America.

OUR COMMITMENT TO OUR CUSTOMERS

Figurines lined up for dressing.

Dear Sir,

Thank you so much for repairing my three Carolers. They look great! I also want to thank you for returning them before Christmas. I now have a collection of ten and am very proud of them.

Sincerely,
Debbie Freed

Byers' Choice is committed to offering a quality product at a fair price. It is important that each employee buys into this philosophy, because the Byers family feels it would be impossible to produce the caroling figurines without this commitment to their customers.

Dressing the Gardener.

A VICTORIAN FAMILY

Perhaps because the figures are handmade, those who own them seem to have a special relationship, not only with their chosen pieces, but also with Byers' Choice. Customers feel they know the Byers family personally, so the commitment becomes like that between friends. This commitment is demonstrated in many ways. Cheerful customer service representatives are instructed to settle a complaint in any way the customer feels is fair. Each year hundreds of broken figures are returned with letters telling of basement floods or family pets with a taste for rabbit fur, who destroyed a part of the family's Christmas traditions. Whenever possible, these figures are restored and returned to their owners at no charge.

If there is an ice storm in New England or a flood in California, Bob will call stores to determine if there is any way Byers' Choice can help. Depending on the needs, replacement product may be sent immediately at no charge, or outstanding bills may be erased. Bob will also try to contact customers to let them know they are in the prayers of the Byers' Choice company—and family.

Dear Sir or Madam:

On 11-29-97, I sent a defective clock back to you for repair and/or replacement. On this date (12-8-97) I received a replacement clock in the mail with no questions asked. I would like to express my thanks and appreciation for your prompt service. It is gratifying to know that there are still companies like yours that place their customers first. Thanks again.

Sincerely yours,
Yvonne Ferraro

To Whom It May Concern:

Thank you!!

I came home Friday evening and found my six "like new" Carolers waiting for me. I cannot thank you enough for the wonderful job you did of repairing what I thought was a total loss. The miracle you performed on some of them was unbelievable. I am still amazed. It gives me a wonderful feeling to know that there is at least one company out there that provides such great customer service. I have not stopped talking about it.

I hope each and everyone has a most joyous holiday season. You all have certainly made mine.

Sincerely,
Katherine M. McCormack

PART TWO

Our Favorite Carolers from the Past Twenty Years

CHRISTMAS MEANS THE SPIRIT OF GIVING, PEACE AND JOY TO YOU,

THE GOODNESS OF LOVING, THE GLADNESS OF LIVING,

THESE ARE CHRISTMAS, TOO.

SO KEEP CHRISTMAS WITH YOU ALL THROUGH THE YEAR,

WHEN CHRISTMAS IS OVER, SAVE SOME CHRISTMAS CHEER,

THESE PRECIOUS MOMENTS, HOLD THEM VERY DEAR,

AND KEEP CHRISTMAS WITH YOU, ALL THROUGH THE YEAR.

YES, KEEP CHRISTMAS WITH YOU ALL THROUGH THE YEAR.

FROM *"KEEP CHRISTMAS WITH YOU ALL THROUGH THE YEAR"*
BY SAM POTTLE AND DAVID AXELROD

Chapter Three

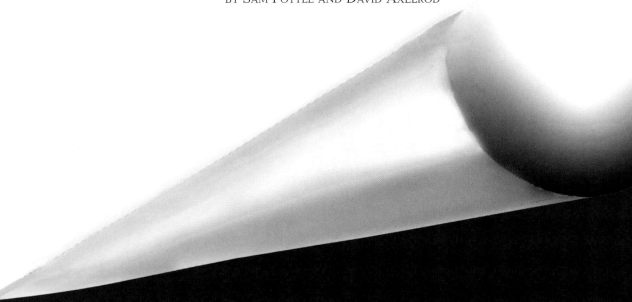

Christmas Around the World

BAVARIAN BOY (1993) and WEIHNACHTSMANN (GERMAN SANTA) (1990)

The Christmas season is a time for celebration and joy over the birth of the Christ child, as well as a universal time for strengthening family ties and for giving. There are so many different ways to celebrate this wonderful time of year. All around the world, in different climates, with people of various races, backgrounds, and cultures, Christmas celebrations utilize unique traditions and customs.

It's wonderful to see that the special feeling of the Christmas season is shared across the globe. The universal spirit of giving and a variety of Christmas stories inspired Joyce to create the characters featured in this chapter.

One of the mainstays of Christmas is the poinsettia plant with its bright-red flower that blooms only in December, which was introduced to the United States in 1825 from Mexico. Mexican legends about the poinsettia abound, but one of the most popular is that of a girl who came to Jesus' manger during the annual Christmas pageant celebrated in her village. On her way into the church, she picked some greens from a nearby bush. After she laid them at the manger, they suddenly bloomed into the vibrant red flower. In Mexico, the plants are called *la Flor de Nochebuena*, the Flower of the Holy Night. To commemorate Mexico's gift to the world, Joyce created a Mexican girl and boy, featured opposite.

Although St. Lucia was an Italian maiden, she has come to be identified by Swedes everywhere as the saint who released them from a terrible famine in the fourth century. According to legend, when Lucia's mother lay dying, Lucia vowed to dedicate her life to the Lord if he would spare her mother's life. When her mother lived, Lucia kept her promise by bringing food and drink to Christians hiding from their persecutors in the catacombs in the outskirts of Sicily. She wore a wreath of lighted candles in her hair, which allowed her to find her way through the darkness while leaving her hands free to carry her basket of food. A pagan nobleman fell in love with the beautiful Lucia, but when she rejected his advances, he turned her over to the authorities, who blinded her, so she could no longer find her way to the caves. The Lord restored her sight, and as a result, she was martyred by angry town leaders. Swedish Vikings brought this legend back to their homes, where their

(continued on page 48)

MEXICAN CHILDREN (1997)

What Inspires Joyce's Carolers... and What Makes Them So Collectible?

The inspiration for Joyce's Carolers comes from so many sources. She might be inspired by a face she sees in the grocery store or in church. Other times, she is inspired by stories and traditions.

Sometimes the inspiration comes from the outside, when Joyce is asked by a charity or other organization to design a figure to commemorate a special event or milestone.

This was the case with Peddler's Village, a group of shops and restaurants that has become a noted Bucks County tourist attraction over the past thirty years. Joyce was approached by the Village's owners to make a signature figurine for their anniversary. She felt a figure of a peddler carrying his wares—as wide a variety as he could carry—was most appropriate, and the Peddler's Village Peddler was born.

PEDDLER'S VILLAGE PEDDLER (1997)

Above left: One of the most endearing specialty characters in the Byers' Choice line was the DRUMMER BOY (1982–1992). Above right: The figure was inspired by this pastel illustration, which was created by Joyce's mother.

No two Caroler figurines are alike and only one hundred of each figure is ever created. According to Joyce, this is one of the most difficult ideas for people to grasp. Because of the variation in eye color, material used for a jacket or dress, or even position in which the character is posed, a vast number of different figures are made. Rarely will two of the same character be sent to a store, so if you buy a woman and plan to go back a week later to purchase her mate, you will probably be disappointed to find him gone—and have no way of ordering another. While this may sometimes be frustrating to the consumer, this diversity is part of what makes Byers' Choice Caroler figurines truly unique and collectible.

ST. LUCIA (1996–)

countrymen were starving. After they began to pray to her, the famine was broken. And with that success, a tradition was born.

The feast of St. Lucia is celebrated in Sweden and throughout the world by those of Swedish ancestry, with a special custom. On the morning of December 13, the oldest daughter in each family puts on a long white robe with a white sash, and wears a wreath with seven candles on her head. She delivers *lussekatter* (raisin buns) and coffee to each member of her family before they get out of bed to symbolize the devout Lucia who brought food to the hungry Christians. The St. Lucia figurine is featured above.

Children of Italy celebrate the Christmas season by awaiting Old Befana. On the evening of January 5, they set out their shoes in anticipation of her arrival and the candy and gifts with which she fills the shoes.

As the legend goes, the three Wise Men came upon Old Befana on their way to view the

Christ Child in Bethlehem. Befana, being busy sweeping her floors, ignored their queries about the child and directions to the city, brushing them away as she brushed away the dirt from her home. Soon after she dismissed them, she began to feel guilty about sending them off, so she packed up some gifts (cakes and candies) to take to the newborn Holy Child. She grabbed her broom, which she intended to use to clean his room, and set out on her own quest for the Christ Child. Because she set out late, however, Befana missed the guiding star and had trouble finding the child, so she decided to visit each small child in Italy, in case he or she was the one for whom the three Wise Men were searching.

Befana, whose name comes from the word Epiphany, the season of the Church immediately following Christmas, is generally characterized as a witch in Italian folklore. When she comes into the children's rooms, they must be sleeping. If the youngsters are awake, she won't leave gifts. To be sure they are actually sleeping, it is said that Old Befana will tickle the bottoms of the children's feet, and if they giggle, she will leave. Kids around the country can be found practicing holding in their giggles while brothers and sisters tickle their feet, in preparation for the visit from the old witch.

Dear Mr. and Mrs. Byers,
Your Carolers are a source of joy in our household. Setting them up and creating stories about them is something my teenage daughter and I love doing together. Her favorite is Old Befana and mine is the Choir Directress.
Thank you for all that you both do to make the world a better place for others—and for the Carolers that light up so many lives!

Sincerely,
Edie Faile

OLD BEFANA (1994–)

Joyce Remembers

When Bob and I established our own Christmas traditions, they were modest. We purchased our first tree at an everything-must-go sale. Just two days after Christmas, the tree fell over and broke the few balls we had hung on it.

We have never put an emphasis on gifts. As the boys were growing up, we encouraged them to make gifts. Frequently they were given gifts of family participation, such as tickets to a magic show or sports event. As the boys grew, we began to celebrate Christmas as it would be celebrated in other countries. We would eat a typical Christmas meal from that country as well as exchange gifts following its traditions, and several years ago we began to travel to other countries during the Christmas season to participate in other customs firsthand.

Gift giving in our family has remained symbolic. Each adult family member and guest brings a wrapped gift, with a value of no more than fifty dollars, which would be suitable for all. Then everyone chooses a gift. Over the years it has been great fun to see how creative in mind and talent each participant can be.

Our tree is a family treasure. Ornaments from the various countries we have visited are hung on it. Camels from Egypt hang next to Wedgwood from England. Also, many of the ornaments have been made by us or our crafty friends. Redware animals and tin angels, glass-etched snowflakes and quilted squares share branches with a paper ornament that Bob or Jeff made in the Boy Scouts.

St. Patrick's Day would most likely be the first holiday to spring to mind when one hears the word "Ireland." Although the birthday of this patron saint of Ireland is celebrated on March 17, Christmas is another holiday associated with St. Patrick, as he was the one who introduced Christmas to the Irish. It was in the fifth century that this Christian tradition was first observed in Ireland. Ever since, they have celebrated in ways which show their strict devotion to the religious and spiritual aspects of the Christmas season.

One Irish Christmas tradition is the placing of lighted candles in each window of the home. As legend has it, the candles are meant to symbolize a welcome to Mary and Joseph, who searched for shelter on the first Christmas Eve. Another story says, however, that the candles show Jesus the homes of his followers. Another unique Irish custom is the placing of raisin and caraway-seed bread and milk along with a candle on the kitchen table as a show of hospitality, both to the Baby Jesus and to any friends who might stop by. The candle

IRISH GIRL (1994)

represents the Baby Jesus and is lit by the youngest child in the family.

A third custom, a secular one, is enacted on St. Stephen's Day, December 26. Irish men and boys, and sometimes girls, go from house to house wearing masks and carrying a straw bird. At each doorstep, they sing and dance to get a gift of pennies. We also can thank the Irish for the custom of placing holly wreaths with their bright red berries in our homes for decoration during the Christmas season. The tradition was brought to America in the nineteenth century, when thousands of Irish people left their homeland to escape the ravages of the Irish Potato Famine. Joyce's Irish Girl is featured on page 51.

Based on a Russian folk story, Dyedt Moroz was not originally associated with the Christmas season, but eventually became so because of his beard and sleigh. According to the story, Dyedt magically turned a wicked Siberian girl into a pillar of ice as punishment for her misbehavior. At the same time, he rewarded her mistreated but well-behaved step-sister with diamonds. Dyedt Moroz, which means Grandfather Frost, delivers gifts to good children on January 6

to celebrate the New Year. Introduced by Byers' Choice in 1989, the Russian Santa figurine is featured on page 54.

In Germany there are plenty of holiday characters to scare the pants off bad little boys and girls—Knecht Ruprecht and Krampus are just two. But fortunately, German lore also has a host of gift-bearers, such St. Nicholas, Weihnachtsmann, and Kris Kringle.

Our Weihnachtsmann (German Santa) holds a *Tannenbaum* (or Christmas tree), a tradition believed to have begun in Germany. He also carries a bag a fruit and a heart-shaped *lebkuchen*, a gingerbread-like confection usually decorated with colorful icing. In his pack are an assortment of packages, toys, candy and noisemakers—gifts that are sure to delight the little ones. Weihnactsmann is pictured on page 42.

The legend of St. Nicholas began in the third century. As the story goes, Nicholas was caught in a fierce storm while sailing on a ship in the Mediterranean. He prayed to God to calm the storm, and his prayers were answered. Upon landing at Myra (currently Turkey),

(continued on page 55)

ST. NICHOLAS (1988–92), KNECHT RUPRECHT (1988–89), and DUTCH KIDS (1992)

DYEDT MOROZ (RUSSIAN SANTA) (1989)

Nicholas went to the church to thank God for sparing him. At the same time, the church elders were trying to elect a new bishop, and they received a vision that told them to choose the first man named Nicholas who came into the church to pray after a certain hour. Nicholas was immediately elected.

St. Nicholas is known for his kindness and good deeds. One story tells of a small village, where St. Nicholas heard of three girls who could not marry because their poor father couldn't afford their dowries. So the girls secretly drew lots, agreeing that the loser would be sold into slavery to save the other two. Nicholas saved them all by throwing a bag of gold through each girl's window.

St. Nicholas' Eve is celebrated on December 5 in various ways throughout the world. In Holland, Dutch children leave their wooden shoes by the fire hoping to find them filled with goodies in the morning. St. Nicholas travels from home to home on a large, white horse with his elfish companion, Knecht Ruprecht. As the story goes, Knecht slides down the chimney into the house and unlocks the door for St. Nick, who then decides if the child has been good all year—in which case, he or she will receive gifts. But if St. Nick determines that the child hasn't studied his or her catechism and behaved, coal and a switch will be left at the hearth by Knecht. So, his original mission of preparing children's hearts for the celebration of the birth of Christ lives on in Holland today. An imposing duo, Joyce's St. Nicholas and Knecht Ruprecht made their debut in 1988. They are featured on page 53.

Father Christmas (below) is the Victorian Santa that originated in English folklore. Joyce was inspired to design him as a Caroler after discovering a late 1800s postcard in her collection of Christmas cards.

FATHER CHRISTMAS (1991–1992)

Chapter Four

Santa and
Mrs. Claus

VELVET Mrs. CLAUS (1987–) and SANTA (1978–)

HO–HO–HO.

No other repeated syllable has the recognition of this one or inspires the same joyous reaction among children of all ages. Little ones everywhere find the prospect of a visit from Santa Claus to be awe-inspiring, and they exhibit good behavior for weeks before the big night. Actually sitting on Santa's lap has instantly brought more than one chatty child to shy silence.

"His eyes how they twinkled; his dimples how merry...and he shook when he laughed like a bowl full of jelly."

With those now-famous words by Clement C. Moore, in his immortal poem, "A Visit from St. Nicholas," the "jolly old elf" known as St. Nicholas has traveled through the years as an all-knowing Christmas-time friend of the well-behaved. Dr. Moore, a Bible Studies professor who wrote the poem as a gift for his children in 1822, didn't intend for it to be published. But after a friend submitted it to a newspaper in Troy, New York, in 1823, Dr. Moore's image of Santa spread. By the late 1800s, the famous cartoonist Thomas Nast developed St. Nicholas into the Santa we know today.

Portrayed as a chubby, white-bearded, kindly old gentleman, Santa is dressed in a white, fur-trimmed red jacket and trousers with matching cap. A wide leather belt encircles his belly and he wears leather boots. On his back he carries a large bag filled to overflowing with gifts. Even though this sack should be heavy and cumbersome, Santa carries the burden as if it were as light as a feather. Santa Claus has been known by a variety of names, and his appearance has varied in his different incarnations around the world.

The first Byers' Choice Santas appeared on the scene in the early 1970s. The Old World Santa, or Belsnickle, was one of these earliest Santa figurines. In Joyce's design, Belsnickle is a combination of the character popular in Victorian England and the more imposing one brought to the New World from Europe with the Pennsylvania Dutch.

The Christmas custom among the Pennsylvania Dutch of the 1700s involved the fearsome Belsnickle. He would burst into homes on Christmas Eve, dressed in ragged clothing and furs, shaking sleigh bells and rattles and cracking a buggy whip. Children, frightened of the noise and of his appearance, which included a face blackened by burnt cork, would run and hide in fear. He would command them to tell him if they had been naughty or nice and would then scatter nuts and candies on the floor. As they scampered around, picking up the goodies, he would crack his whip

(continued on page 63)

**TWENTIETH ANNIVERSARY BELSNICKLE (1998) and
ORIGINAL BELSNICKLE (OLD WORLD SANTA) (1978–86)**

Joyce Remembers:
A Byers' Family Christmas

Last Christmas, during the bedlam that ensued as four children under the age of four opened their packages, the conversation turned to memories of Christmases past.

Weeks before Christmas, there would be a lot of whispering and closed doors as gifts were made for each member of the family. Jeff recalled making a fort for Bobby's G.I. Joe. Bobby remembered the bird feeder he made for the family. Both had many memories of the space ship Bob constructed from a large cardboard cylinder. Jeff would search the house for presents, whereas Bobby enjoyed surprises.

Christmas Eve we would settle in as we built a fire in the fireplace and put up the tree. The boys had made many of the ornaments and enjoyed unwrapping them and hanging them year after year. Toy soldiers and animals cut from felt and decorated with beads and glitter were among their favorites. A large wooden bowl was kept filled with popcorn for both snacking and stringing. Nutcrackers were unboxed and put to the test of nut cracking. When the tinsel was finally hung and the lights were lit, we would all sit back and agree that it was the most beautiful tree we had ever seen. A Christmas story was read before the stockings were hung, and two excited little boys would climb the steps to bed.

Christmas morning began at 6:00 A.M., but needless to say, everyone was already up. At the first strike of the clock, we would scurry down the steps to see what Santa had brought for us.

VICTORIAN TODDLERS (1995)

WORKING SANTA, first edition (1983–91) and Mrs. CLAUS ON ROCKER (1986)

**WORKING SANTA, second edition
(1992–1996)**

again and demand they recite Bible verses. Then he would be gone as quickly and with as much commotion as when he had arrived.

By the late 1800s, the early Belsnickle character had softened. The custom of portraying Belsnickle had combined with a tradition brought by Episcopalians from England called mumming. Mummers would dress in costumes and masks and make their way from home to home on Christmas Eve performing plays. For their efforts, they were paid with drink, sweets, and coins. Toward the end of the nineteenth century, the groups had become organized and in some areas formed parades. In the Philadelphia area, the Mummers Parade is a famous trademark of New Year's Day. Mummers costumes have become increasingly elaborate, adding feathers and large masks. Some of the costumes are intended to depict a wide variety of characters.

Joyce designed her Belsnickle figure with that combination of characters in mind. Therefore, he is dressed similarly to a Victorian Santa, but carries bells and switches like the eighteenth-century Dutch character to remind youngsters that they must earn the goodies he brings them. Belsnickle is featured on page 59.

As every child knows, Santa Claus must work hard all year round in his workshop to have just

Dear Bob, Joyce, Lisa, Patty & Debbie,

Thank you all for the lovely lunch on Saturday. It was a wonderful visit, and it's always a highlight to see each and every one of you. You all in your own way make all the collectors feel very, very special. I really look forward to my visits there.

Oh, and my gorgeous display Santa!! How I love him. It's as if he were custom made for me. I have gorgeous blue families to match him. I'll send pictures at Christmastime.

Wreath Lady is awesome and so are you folks. I wish you could all visit my home so I could reciprocate the hospitality.

Love,
Heather

the right toys and gifts ready for his worldwide journey on Christmas Eve. Key to his preparation is the list he makes up and checks twice. Every good boy and girl can be assured of receiving a gift from Santa, and anyone who finds their name on his naughty list may find coal in his or her stocking on Christmas morning.

The Working Santa (see pages 62–63) has gone through various styles since his introduction in 1983. Throughout the years, his costume of a gray work shirt, red pants, and suspenders has remained largely unchanged, as he has been hard at work checking a long, scrolled list with his white quill pen (first edition), or painting the final touches on a toy rocking horse (second edition).

In 1984 and 1985, a display-size Working Santa was offered. About three feet tall, the only other difference from the smaller version was that his list rolled down to his feet, which were now shod in slippers rather than boots. The epitome of Santa's Workshop can be seen in the museum at Byers' Choice headquarters in Chalfont, Pennsylvania. Santa and Mrs. Claus work alongside scores of elves and other Carolers to create just the right toys and trinkets for good little boys and girls around the world.

Mrs. Claus, a sweet-faced grandmotherly woman, appeared in 1984. The first female Santa figure, she wore a lace-trimmed red dress and white apron, and has worn this outfit through the years, only changing the types of accessories she holds, including tiny teddy bears, books, and toy-filled stockings.

In 1986, a special Mrs. Claus was produced (see page 62). Happily seated in a rocker and surrounded by toys, Mrs. Claus reads a Christmas book. The whole scene is mounted on a wooden

base. About two hundred feature a small child in a nightgown sitting on Mrs. Claus' lap.

Another special Mrs. Claus, introduced in 1995, sings while she puts the finishing touches on her latest work of needlepoint. Set inside her miniature embroidery hoop, the muslin reads "Home Sweet Home," printed above a picture of her little North Pole house. This Mrs. Claus is featured above right.

In an attempt to humanize the couple, Joyce has created several Santa figurines performing routine tasks. One of these designs,

created in 1997, shows Mrs. Claus making her way home after spending the day shopping for gifts—perhaps something special for Santa and the elves—as she peers over an armful of festively wrapped packages.

In 1992, a second edition of the Working Couple was introduced, in which Santa is busy putting the finishing touches on a special toy, while Mrs. Claus tries to wrap up her gift for Santa without being caught (above left).

Santa may feel that proper care and feeding of his magical reindeer is too important a

Left: Mrs. CLAUS, second edition, (1992–1993) with TRADITIONAL TEENS and BOY.

Right: Mrs. CLAUS NEEDLEWORK (1995)

SANTA FEEDING REINDEER (1997)

task to entrust to a subordinate. So in 1997, a Santa Feeding Reindeer figurine was introduced, in which Santa holds a sack of reindeer food and offers some in one outstretched hand to a four-legged member of the Christmas team.

The Knickerbocker Santa (right), designed by Joyce in 1996, is based on an illustration by T.C. Boyd, a wood engraver, who reinforced the flavor of Dutch New York in a series of engravings he made for C.C. Moore's "A Visit from St. Nicholas." Boyd's figure was an elfin creature wearing knickers. Joyce's decision to name the figure "Knickerbocker" came from a combination of the knee pants worn by early Dutch settlers and the nickname given them by American writer Washington Irving. Knickerbocker Santa wears knickers and buckled shoes, and he holds a Dutch pipe in one hand and a bag of toys in the other.

No matter what we may call our version of Santa Claus or how we imagine him to look, he is a constant and important part of the American Christmas celebration, reminding boys and girls of all ages that the receipt of special gifts is a privilege to be earned.

As Santa says, "Merry Christmas to all, and to all a good night!"

**KNICKERBOCKER SANTA (1996–) and
TODDLER WITH BOOK (1996–)**

Chapter Five

Charles Dickens' London

THE CRATCHITS

A Christmas Carol

Christmas is not only a time for Santa, gifts, trees, and merriment. The Christmas season carries with it a deeper sense of purpose, of sharing our blessings, of giving to those less fortunate, and of reliving the years past—both good and bad—and looking ahead with anticipation.

Giving doesn't come easy to a lot of people. Many are more interested in what they get out of life than what they put into it. Charles Dickens did an outstanding job identifying this in his character, Scrooge. As you know, it was the Spirit, or Spirits, of Christmas who enabled Scrooge to first see the need for giving, and helped him dip into his pocket and share with his fellow man.

Christmas gives us all this opportunity. Whether we bake cookies for an elderly neighbor, drop a few coins into a Salvation Army kettle, or make a special effort to find just the right gift for someone we love, the act of giving to others is very rewarding.

The closing lines of *A Christmas Carol* read, "...it was always said of [Scrooge] that he knew how to keep Christmas well, if any man alive possessed that knowledge. May that be truly said of us, and all of us! And may so as Tiny Tim observed, 'God bless us, every one.'"

Joyce approached the Dickens line as a challenge and an opportunity. She remembers: "We first introduced Scrooge in 1983, thinking that Bob and Mrs. Cratchit and Tiny Tim would join Scrooge in succeeding years as they each had a lesson to teach. Scrooge, and indeed, the whole line, was so well received that we introduced second editions of them all.

"My earliest characters had even more exaggerated faces than those of today, perhaps because I, like Dickens, look for the story behind each person. Dickens' time was not perfect, and he didn't write about beautiful people. He enjoyed his characters, many of whom were from the lower strata of society, for their personalities. The public, however, remembers the Victorian era as romantic, so I adapted the faces of my figurines to better suit their tastes. For me, Scrooge was the antithesis of this look, and an opportunity to present the more spiritual aspect of the holiday."

The first edition Scrooge is one of the few Carolers to have clay hands. He wears a white nightshirt, solid red long johns, brown felt slippers, and red nightcap with unruly gray hair sprouting from beneath it. Although he was an undeniably unattractive figure, this Scrooge sold very well.

The second edition Scrooge wears a similar outfit, but holds a candlestick in his mitten-wrapped hands. His red long johns have been changed to a red and white striped pattern, and he has clay feet.

The Happy Scrooge, introduced in 1991, is truly a changed man. On his face he wears a look of ecstatic amazement. This redeemed character dances gaily on one foot and carries packages, a basket of bright red poinsettias, and a walking stick. His gray cloak is tied with a smart plaid ribbon, marking him as a dashing

HAPPY SCROOGE (1991–1992)

man about town. But perhaps the most noticeable difference is the wide and genuinely happy smile upon his face.

Mrs. Cratchit joined Scrooge in 1984 as the second Dickens character. She wore the dark clothing of a working woman—plaid apron, dark shawl, and white blouse—and carried a plum pudding in her hands. When the first Mrs. Cratchit's apron was made, Joyce saved a few yards of the fabric to use for patches on Bob Cratchit's trousers. She never dreamed that she would need so many patches. The few yards she saved patched only the first several thousand pairs of pants. So keep your eyes open— perhaps you might find a Bob Cratchit whose pants are patched with the material from Mrs. Cratchit's original apron.

The Mr. and Mrs. Fezziwig Carolers are as jolly as they were in the Dickens tale. The Fezziwigs, introduced in 1985, were some of the first figures to stand or dance on one foot. While Joyce loved their movement, the problem was, just as with the jolly folks they depicted, that the figures became tipsy and would topple over more easily than a figurine with two feet firmly planted on the ground. Their merriment was so vital to the characters, however, that the Byers' Choice artists simply used additional care to help

MARLEY'S GHOST (1986–92) and SCROOGE (1983–)

the figures maintain their balance. After many queries from collectors wondering who the Fezziwigs were, the Byers decided to publish their own version of *A Christmas Carol* in 1989. Using the original text by Charles Dickens, Byers' Choice added pages of photographs of the Caroler figurines acting out the popular story.

Jacob Marley's character, as described by Dickens, was transparent. This presented a design challenge for Joyce, who at first considered using Lucite and gauze to achieve this see-through effect. While apprenticing with his mother the year before he started college, Jeff discovered the key to creating Marley's Ghost in his true spirit—he used many shades of gray. Marley was wrapped in brass bells and chains. Many collectors liked the bells and thought they made Marley look more realistic, while others removed them for storage to prevent rusting. To make this character even more realistic, Joyce wrapped Marley's chin with a chin strap. In Dickens' story, Marley's Ghost is

Left: THE FEZZIWIGS (1985–1990)

Right: SPIRITS OF CHRISTMAS PAST (1987–91), PRESENT (1988–91), and FUTURE (1989–91)

described as having a folded kerchief bound about his head and chin. In Victorian times, the dead had their chins bound like this to keep their mouths from falling open.

The Spirit of Christmas Past was the first of the three spirits to be introduced. Dickens described him as a child or an old man, so a child figurine was used. The first edition wore a white tunic trimmed with white flowers, and in the second, yellow flower trim was substituted, which accentuated the unruly yellow hair used to simulate the light emanating from his head. A sprig of holly and berries held in one hand added a dash of color to this otherworldly figure, while he carried a snuffer with which to extinguish the light in the other hand.

The jovial Spirit of Christmas Present wore a green velveteen gown, tied with a gold rope belt and trimmed with brown fur when he was introduced in 1988, and carried a cornucopia under one arm, while raising a golden goblet with the other hand. In the second edition, released in 1989, he carried a burning torch instead of the goblet.

The Spirit of Christmas Future required a change in design from its debut in 1989. Pointing the way to the gravestone engraved "Ebenezer Scrooge" with one bony clay finger didn't work out because Joyce originally used the wrong type of clay, requiring innumerable repairs. In the second edition, the clay hand was replaced by a mitten-wrapped one. Because of his gloomy appearance—he appears in a black robe with his face hidden by a hood—Joyce was amazed that the Spirit of Christmas Future was so well received. He is also the only Caroler figurine with no face. In 1989, when the apparition first appeared, collectors commented, "I can't believe I'm buying this." Now they tell Joyce, "I use him as a Halloween decoration."

The long-awaited Bob Cratchit and Tiny Tim finally arrived in 1990. The long-suffering, yet happy child carried on his loving father's back is a favorite of collectors.

Joyce hoped this series of Carolers would encourage people to read *A Christmas Carol* and think about the joy that comes from giving and sharing. Because, as she says, "Christmas has always been about giving. God gave his greatest gift in the form of the Baby Jesus, and the Wise Men traveled far to give him gifts of gold, frankincense, and myrrh. Throughout the ages gifts have been given at Christmas time. May we always keep in mind the joys of the season, and live the spirit of giving."

STREET PEOPLE OF LONDON

In Victorian London, there was no shortage of vendors peddling their wares in the streets. Products were offered by butchers, bakers, candlestick makers, and sellers of every imaginable type of food. Many of these street people of London found their way into in the Cries of London series introduced by Joyce in 1991. Long interested in these itinerants, she discovered that adding these characters to her Victorian and Traditional Carolers enabled her to add a more lifelike feel to the street scenes through the sheer variety of characters. In addition, possibilities for expansion of the line are virtually endless. The Cries allowed Joyce to pursue her interest in

CANDLESTICK MAKER, WOMAN SELLING CANDLES, and CHILDREN WITH CANDLES (1998–)

Clockwise: ONE MAN BAND (1997–)

BUTCHER (1995)

CONSTABLE (1994–96)

BOY WITH GOOSE (1994–95)

these people from the past. Slightly different than the figurines which preceded them, the Cries didn't concentrate on the Christmas connection, rather, they brought a bit of historical connection and diversity to the growing list of Carolers.

The first of the Cries characters introduced was the Apple Lady. Seated on a bench, she gaily cries out the word of her wares for sale— shiny red apples lined neatly in a box on her lap. She represents the vendors who populated the streets of London during the late 1800s, who were also known as costermongers.

The Apple Lady was extremely popular, and demand for her exceeded supply. According to sales rep, Bob Watson, "Everybody felt comfortable with her and we couldn't deliver enough of them." Since the Cries are produced for only one year each, many collectors were disappointed when the end of 1991 signaled the retirement of this apple-cheeked favorite. The Apple Lady can be found wearing either solid red or red-and-white striped stockings, three different skirt fabrics, and holding different baskets or crates for her apples. These variations in style depended strictly on fabric and accessory availability.

When working with Byers' Choice Carolers, one never knows when one will come

APPLE LADY (1991)

across a touching and emotional story relating to the figurines and those who collect them. "One of the most moving stories concerning the Carolers that I have ever been told was about a young woman, her mother, and an Apple Lady. It seems that the young woman's father had passed away, leaving her mother completely distraught…so distraught that she could not participate in any projects around the house that reminded her of her loss, including the decorating and celebrating of Christmas. As I recall, the daughter found an Apple Lady and thought her mother would enjoy it due to the

BAKER (1992)

fact that orchards surrounded the land around her house. The mother was so enchanted with the Apple Lady that she and her daughter made trips to see other pieces that Byers' Choice had made. Inspired by the Christmas joy in the faces of the Carolers, her mother was able to celebrate Christmas and enjoy the season for the first time in many years."

The Candlestick Maker was obviously kept very busy before the invention of the oil lamp, gas lamp, and finally, electricity. It is difficult for us to imagine a world two hundred years ago lit only by candles. The Candlestick Maker sells candlesticks made of brass and tin, and carries a candelabra in one hand.

A vendor wouldn't be in business for very long if she or he didn't have any customers for their wares. So Joyce began creating Traditional Carolers to accompany the Cries. They may be children or shoppers holding one of whatever the seller has to offer. Children holding apples in their hands were produced, as were figurines holding bread, dolls, gingerbread cookies, chestnuts, flowers, and candles.

"Hot cross buns!" the bakery vendor cried aloud. The man selling fresh bread would be a welcome sight to the hungry person on the street. Even children today recognize the song "Hot cross buns, hot cross buns, one a penny, two a penny, hot cross buns." This cry was used only on Good Friday morning, but nevertheless became a popular song for Victorian children along with another about a baker: "Oh, do you know the muffin man, the muffin man, the muffin man? Oh, do you know the muffin man who lives in Drury Lane?" The aroma of freshly baked bread and cakes, still warm from the oven, must have permeated the streets, and brought the hungry from blocks around. These vendors carried their wares on trays held by straps over their shoulders or on their heads. Each baker in town, or "cake man" as he was also called, specialized in baking one type of bread, and the muffin men, or vendors, would buy from various bakers so they could offer a variety of goodies out on the streets.

The Baker's hands—and head—are full of his fresh wares, with a basket under his arm and another perched atop his head. He is dressed in clean baker's white, and sports a large furry mustache, a change of pace for the male figurines, who up to this point, had had facial hair sculpted into their clay faces and then painted.

The distinctive fragrance of roasting chestnuts has inspired at least one contemporary Christmas song and undoubtedly has whetted countless appetites as it wafts through the air.

MAN ROASTING CHESTNUTS (1993)

FLOWER VENDOR (1994)

The Chestnut Roaster is depicted as an elderly man, slightly stooped by the years and his labors. Joyce fondly remembers the chestnut roasters in the wintertime streets of Philadelphia, as well as those she has seen in London and Vienna. With his warm green jacket and his head protected from the cold in a plum-colored velvet cap complete with feather,

the Chestnut Roaster seems to say that he takes great pride in offering his tasty treat.

Bringing a bit of springtime to a wintry day is the Flower Vendor. Dressed neatly in a soft red jacket that brings out the auburn of her hair, this lovely young woman carries a full basket of sweet-smelling blooms over each arm, while handing out a bunch in one hand. The flower girls of Victorian London were often young Irish women who cried out, "Flowers 'ere, penny a bunch!" Joyce chose to introduce the Flower Vendor in 1994. (The Bucks Beautiful Flower Vendor was based on this figurine, and was designed to promote the community beautification program started by Bob and Joyce and presently run by the Central Bucks Chamber of Commerce. See page 21 for more information.)

The real street criers always had to have tricks up their sleeves in order to make a sale. The doll maker was no exception. According to one doll vendor (as reported to Henry Mayhew, a chronicler of Victorian London), compliments to the young customer and her parent, guardian, or nursemaid were invaluable for securing a sale.

"Spoiled children are our best customers," said the unidentified vendor. "Whenever we sees a likely customer approaching, we—that is, those who know their business—always

DOLL MAKER (1995) and GIRLS HOLDING DOLL (1995)

GINGERBREAD VENDOR (1996)

Dolls made from leftover scraps of clothing and bits of yarn and thread were common among young Victorian girls, and the 1995 Doll Maker carries an assortment of these little ones—known as penny or ha'penny dolls because of their low cost—in her basket. Since Joyce imagined that an older woman, a former seamstress perhaps, had begun to create the tiny dolls from scraps of fabric left over from years of sewing, this figurine is gray-haired with a somewhat careworn appearance. The tiny wire spectacles perched on the end of her nose may be just the thing to better help her spot the indulged child who will buy her next little doll.

When the Gingerbread Vendor, fashioned after a well-known peddler of gingerbread in Victorian London known as the Tiddy Diddy Doll, was introduced in 1996, the staff at Byers' Choice were forced to endure the wonderful aroma of baking cookies, as most of the cookie accessories were baked in the company kitchen adjacent to the customer service offices. It was probably fortunate that these cookies were not edible. The vendor's unusual nickname came from the song he sang as part of the act he performed to attract customers, "Tiddy Diddy Doll, lol, lol, lol." The

throw ourselves in the way and spread out our dolls to the best advantage. If we hears young miss say she will have one, and cries for it, we are almost sure of a customer, and if we sees her kick and fight a bit with the nuss-maid, we are sure of a good price." (Excerpted from *Mayhew's London*, 1951.)

MILKMAID (1997)

Gingerbread Vendor was referred to as the king of the itinerant street peddlers, and dressed the part in a ruffled shirt, fancy suit, and silk stockings.

Before the age of refrigeration or iceboxes, the citizens of London relied on the services of the milkmaid to provide them with fresh milk. The milkmaids were a hardy lot as they carried their product in heavy tin pails from the cow-houses to the streets in search of customers. In spite of their backbreaking labors, they tended to be a cheerful and strong group of young women, carrying up to 130 pounds for two or more miles. Joyce's Milkmaid was created with the healthy, fresh complexion and shining golden hair drinking fresh milk would induce.

Folks of all types abounded in Dickens' London. One of several other street characters who found his way into Joyce's imagination and then onto the production floor is the Lamplighter. Although gas lamps were available earlier, it wasn't until about 1825 that the city of London had gas pipelines installed along the streets, which created a ready supply of safe and efficient lighting for homes, businesses, and streets. Before this time, the lamplighter was a common sight along the

dusky streets of the city. He would prop his ladder up on a lamppost, climb to the top, and, adding some oil and trimming the wick, would light the way for shoppers and strollers. Joyce's Lamplighter, introduced in 1993, wears a warm, green coat and black hat, with his head and neck wrapped snugly in a long, red scarf as he goes about his business of illumination.

One other Victorian character who made a special debut in 1994 was the Sandwich Board Man. Think of the Sandwich Board Man as a walking advertisement. With his body sandwiched between two pieces of wood, which were inscribed with everything from ads for shops to announcements of coming events to results of local political elections, he received his name from a description by Charles Dickens, who commented that these men were like "a piece of human flesh between two slices of pasteboard."

"The other night I was reflecting back upon our past twenty years with the Carolers and trying to fully comprehend the incredible experience we have

Left: LAMPLIGHTER (1993–1996)

Right: SANDWICH BOARD MAN (1994–96)

been part of. Suddenly, as if God were speaking to me, I realized the following:

When people sing carols they are doing that which is pleasing to God: loving Him, glorifying Him, praising Him, appreciating Him. Those who have caroled understand the great joy that flows back from caroling. I believe that many who have never caroled still envision the joy and

peace that comes to one's soul from caroling. Consciously or subconsciously, I believe many people who buy the Carolers are people who desire a loving relationship with their Heavenly Father and feel some fulfillment of that desire through the Carolers. To me, this helps explain why collectors are such nice people."

—BOB BYERS

Left: CONDUCTOR (1982–92)

Right: ACTRESS (1996)

CHIMNEY SWEEP (BOY) (1991–1994)

Chapter Six

Holiday Traditions and Christmas Joy Throughout the Year

CHOIR DIRECTOR (1993–1995)

HOLIDAY TRADITIONS

Christmas in the northeastern part of the United States, where Byers' Choice Ltd. is located, is associated with snow, warm fires, and marshmallows swimming in hot chocolate. For that reason, many of the special characters and traditional figures are participating in cold weather and snow-related activities such as skating, skiing, and making snowmen. Some of the most

TRADITIONAL SHOPPERS (1995–)

MAN FEEDING BIRDS ON BENCH (1997)

popular are the skating figurines. Whether holding their skates or twirling in a graceful spin, the skaters bring out the child in us all.

The Children with Skates figures were introduced in 1988. Joyce's accidental discovery of an antique skate in a Brimfield, Massachusetts, flea market spurred her to design a whole line of characters around this popular wintertime sport. Although Joyce's "find" was dirty and rusty, it was the missing piece to the puzzle. As she brings her imagination to life in her workshop, occasionally a character piece will wait patiently for that one last item or accessory needed to complete her vision. The steel base and wooden upper portion of the skate attached to the foot with sturdy leather ties was the type of skate made popular in the story, *Hans Brinker*, written by Mary Mapes Dodge in 1865. While most of the skaters either wear or carry skates fashioned after this model, some wear the more contemporary boot skates.

Bundled up snugly against the cold, skaters appear in a variety of poses and generations. In 1991, adults took to the ice with a white base depicting the ice and snow associated with their wintry activity. The children followed in 1992, and the whole family was skating together in 1993 when the grandparents joined them.

Whether sailing gracefully across the ice with hands in a furry muff or warm woolen mittens, or perched on a wooden log tying those skates on tightly, a sense of movement and delight exudes from these figurines.

(Continued on page 95)

ADULTS HOLDING SKATES (1995–)

**CHILDREN WITH SKATES (1988–), ADULT SKATERS (1991–94),
and CHILDREN SKATERS (1992–)**

SKATING SANTA (1993)

Other cold weather activities enjoyed by Caroler figurines include skiing, sledding, and sleigh riding. Romantic Victorian couples come in a variety of costumes. Bundled up warmly, they take wintertime rides in wooden sleighs that sit atop curly silver runners. With their cozy woolen blanket tucked around their legs, they could easily be on a journey to deliver a basket of goodies to friends and loved ones.

Children determined not to waste a moment of fun on a snow-covered hill jump on a sled for a wind-whistling, hair-raising trip to the bottom.

These boys and girls are just old enough to be so adventurous, while their younger siblings enjoy their more sedate, but no less fun, activity of building a snowman in the freshly fallen snow. In 1992, the L'il Dickens Toddlers line was introduced. Too young to join their elders in song, these youngsters seem so natural frolicking in the snow. Bundled up tightly against the cold in their brightly colored snowsuits, these little ones perform the snowy day rituals of childhood—building snowmen, sledding, skiing, and of course, catching snowflakes on outstretched tongues.

Left: KIDS HOLDING SKIS (1995–)

Right: COUPLE IN SLEIGH (1995)

BOY WITH LAMB (1996–) and GIRL WITH HOLLY BASKET (1996–1997)

"I recall one Christmas time in particular when a group of young people piled onto a hay wagon which was drawn from home to home as we sang our favorite carols. The clear, starry sky, the smell of smoke from someone's fireplace, and the brisk winter air will always be at the core of my memories of Christmas."

—JOYCE

Traditions faithfully passed on from generation to generation are cherished at Byers' Choice. Strong childhood memories of family gatherings and holidays shared are the

Clockwise: SKATING BOY ON LOG (1993), NEWSBOY WITH BIKE (1989–1992), and GIRL WITH HOOP (1989–1990)

97

Bringing Home the Tree

by Jeff Byers

Of all the trees we have had through the years, the one that I remember most fondly is the first tree that I was allowed to pick. This seemed to be an enormous responsibility for an eleven-year-old boy, but I was ready to face the challenge. I was up at dawn that morning and off into the woods behind our barn. I was certain that the success or failure of that Christmas was riding on my shoulders. I passed over tree after tree for the smallest of defects until finally, after hours of searching, I found the perfect Christmas tree. I quickly chopped it down, lifted the trunk, and began dragging it through the woods and field back to our house.

The entire family was waiting at the kitchen door as I arrived with my trophy in hand. The looks on their faces instantly told me that they were quite surprised with the choice I had made. When I turned around, I discovered a long trail of small pine branches and needles lining my path back into the woods. The perfect Christmas tree was no longer perfect after the trip home. But, no matter, with the help of a few mugs of hot chocolate and lots of freshly baked cookies, we proceeded to decorate one of the most beautiful Christmas trees I had ever seen.

Our Boy with Tree figurine (introduced in 1991) was designed to capture the important Christmas tradition of selecting the tree. We hope that it will help you to remember your first tree and the wonderful magic of Christmas past.

BOY WITH TREE (1991–1994)

building blocks of so much of Joyce's design work. The discovery of a wooden rocking horse which reminded Joyce of one of her family traditions was the basis for one of the few seated Caroler figures. The Girl on a Rocking Horse was introduced in the summer of 1990. The little girl in her bright red velveteen and lace dress holds her teddy bear tightly as they take a ride in the double rocking horse on a bench seat between the matched pair of ponies. For the past one hundred years, a similar rocking horse has been handed down in Joyce's family to the first child born in each generation.

The first seated figurine made was the Boy on a Rocking Horse, crafted in 1983. Again, it was the chance discovery by Joyce and Bob of an appropriate accessory that led to this creation. An antique-looking rocking horse they spotted in 1982 seemed destined to be part of a Byers' Choice figure. Because it was the first time a figurine was seated, new methods of production were required. Instead of teaching the staff the new methods, Joyce decided to make each figurine herself. The bottom of each rocking horse was signed, dated, and numbered and within four months, all three hundred horses were sold.

BOY ON A ROCKING HORSE (1983)

And it just isn't Christmas without the classic, *The Nutcracker*. Ballet companies—from the tiniest dancers to the most seasoned professionals—perform this beloved Christmas ballet every year. First brought to the stage in 1892, the swirling dreamscape has become synonymous with the holiday season and the hope held by girls and boys that they too may discover an enchanted gift under their tree on Christmas morning.

(continued on page 104)

GIRL ON A ROCKING HORSE (1990–1991)

Left to right: MARIE (1993–), LOUISE PLAYING THE PIANO (1995–1996), and FRITZ (1994–1997)

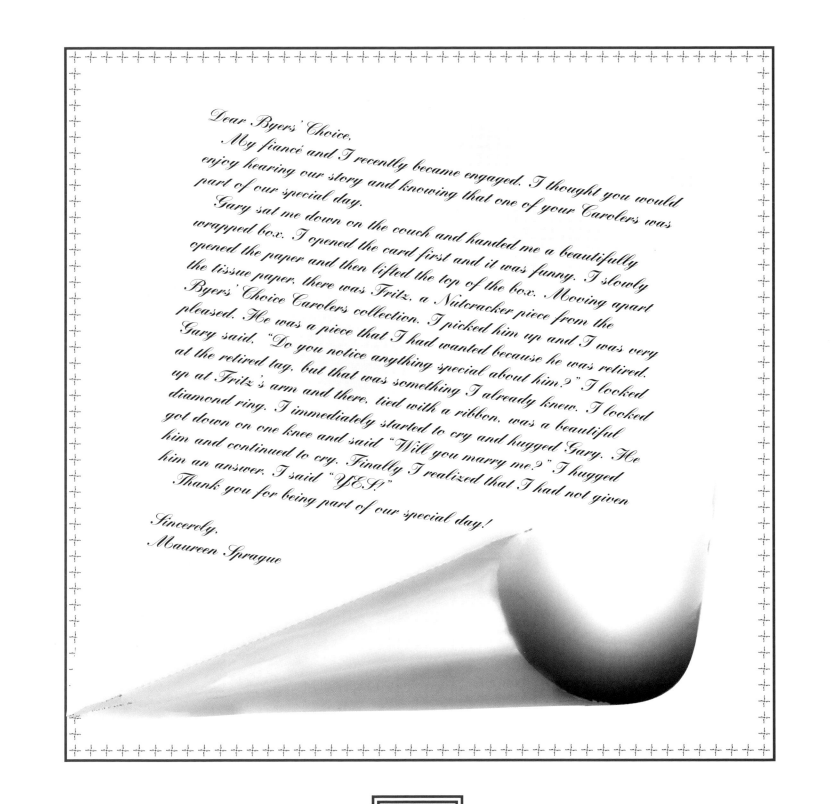

Dear Byers' Choice,

My fiancé and I recently became engaged. I thought you would enjoy hearing our story and knowing that one of your Carolers was part of our special day.

Gary sat me down on the couch and handed me a beautifully wrapped box. I opened the card first and it was funny. I slowly opened the paper and then lifted the top of the box. Moving apart the tissue paper, there was Fritz, a Nutcracker piece from the Byers' Choice Carolers collection. I picked him up and I was very pleased. He was a piece that I had wanted because he was retired. Gary said, "Do you notice anything special about him?" I looked at the retired tag, but that was something I already knew. I looked up at Fritz's arm and there, tied with a ribbon, was a beautiful diamond ring. I immediately started to cry and hugged Gary. He got down on one knee and said "Will you marry me?" I hugged him and continued to cry. Finally I realized that I had not given him an answer. I said "YES!"

Thank you for being part of our special day!

Sincerely,
Maureen Sprague

In her continuing effort to bring a traditional Christmas to life, Joyce decided to create a series of figurines based on the classic story by the German writer E.T.A. Hoffmann, "The Nutcracker and the Mouse King." This tale became the inspiration for Pyotr Ilich Tchaikovsky's wonderful Christmas ballet.

For the series debut in 1993, Joyce created Marie, the young girl transported through time, space, and imagination into a world where toys come to life and all wishes can come true. One can almost hear Marie (who is called Clara in the ballet) singing with delight at being given her shining new toy.

In the story, Marie's brother Fritz is a "typical boy" and almost breaks the nutcracker toy with his rough play. He "fed" the nutcracker "all the biggest and hardest nuts he could find, but all at once there was a 'crack-crack,' and three teeth fell out of Nutcracker's mouth, and his lower jaw became loose and wobbly." Fritz's boyish clatter and noisy fun come fully to life as he gallops across the room on a wooden horse carrying a tiny trumpet. His teal velvet jacket is ringed with a lace collar and the matching cap sports a jauntily placed white feather.

Although the part of Louise, Marie and Fritz's older sister, was a small one in Hoffmann's story,

Joyce felt that adding a Caroler-sized piano with the dainty Louise perched on its bench singing Christmas carols would make a charmingly suitable addition to the growing cast of characters in the Byers' Choice Nutcracker Series. So, in 1995, Joyce created the seated Louise (although there was no piano in the original story), whose cheery pink cheeks and long blond ringlets indelibly mark her as one of the clan.

The "Nutcracker" story would not be complete without Herr Drosselmeier. It is he who brings the enchanted gift of the Nutcracker to the family on Christmas Eve, inspiring Marie's amazing dream. Joyce's design for Drosselmeier closely matches the description given in Hoffmann's "The Nutcracker and the Mouse King." Drosselmeier was "anything but a nice-looking man. He was small and lean, with a great many wrinkles on his face, a big patch of black plaster where his right eye ought to have been, and not a hair on his head; which was why he wore a fine white wig, made of glass..."

While the Byers' Drosselmeier does have a slightly sinister air about him, he holds an elegant music box adorned with a romantic-looking couple, which actually dances. He sports a long cape, white wig, and black eye patch, but the pleasant look on his face belies any evil

DROSSELMEIER WITH MUSIC BOX (1996–)

intent, and shows that he carries the true spirit of Christmas in his heart.

The fifth figurine to become part of the Byers' Nutcracker Series is the Seven-Headed Mouse King. While there is no denying its terrifying nature, Joyce sought to soften its impact. To meet this design challenge, Joyce handed the reins to her talented son, Jeff. "In 'The Nutcracker,' the Mouse King is described as kind of hideous looking," said Jeff. "I wanted to give our Mouse King a friendlier, more capricious look," he added. To that end, he gave this regal-looking king of the rodents a suit of purple and gold and covered him with a cherry red robe. Although he holds a golden sword and attempts to look menacing, his threatening look is softened by a slight upward curve of his lips.

The earliest German Christmas trees were actually bushes without a defined top. Sometimes a candle marked the uppermost branches or a flag or star would be used to decorate the pinnacle. During this time, the Nuremberg gold foil angel was a popular marker, hung in a special spot in the middle of the bush. A large figure, this angel held a

PRINCE (1998–) and SEVEN–HEADED MOUSE KING (1997–)

candle in each hand and stood in the middle of a wreath. Other angels were made of wax, embossed tin, or die-cut colored paper and cardboard. Joyce's Treetop Angel, introduced in 1994, shines in a gauzy white gown with golden wings and has hair like spun gold. Head thrown back in joyous song, she is truly an angelic addition to any Christmas tree.

Left: ANGELS (1987–1991)

Right: TREETOP ANGEL (1994–1996)

◆◆◆

Through the centuries, angels have been associated with the birth of the Christ Child in Bethlehem. An angel appeared to Mary informing her she would deliver the baby and was blessed among women. A host of angels filled the skies the night Jesus was born. To celebrate the Christmas story beloved by Christians around the world, Joyce created a complete Nativity scene— replete with angels. The Caroling angels were the first to make the scene in 1987. The four are distinctly different in appearance, although all are sweet-faced children in long white robes with golden wings and halos. The following year saw the addition of the shepherds and in 1989, the Three Wise Men joined the group. The Nativity was completed in

Nativity from left to right: ANGELS (1987–91)
HOLY FAMILY (1990–91)
WISE MEN (front) (1989–91)
SHEPHERDS (back) (1988–91)

1990, with the addition of Mary, Joseph, and Baby Jesus, along with a stable in which to stage the scene.

CHRISTMAS JOY THROUGHOUT THE YEAR

With all its wonderful pageantry and joyous celebrations, Christmas is a very special time of year for the Byers, and always has been. After all, the very first Caroler figurines ever made were intended as Christmas gifts and were figurines clad in Christmas garb. To Joyce, the Carolers have always been more than just decorations. So, when Byers' Choice sales representatives suggested creating figurines representing other holidays, the idea was met with skepticism.

Joyce reports, "I tried other holidays, but the demand for Christmas decorations was so much greater than the demand for other holidays. It only made sense to concentrate on Christmas. Certainly, we have strayed from this initial theme, but to me the spiritual facet evoked during the Christmas season has been our driving force, and remains our main focus." Although Carolers for minor holidays are no longer being produced, some very magical figurines were made, such as the Valentine's Day and Easter children.

Thanksgiving and Christmas share certain themes of families coming together to share the joys of togetherness and fine food and to think of the past year with thankful remembrance. The two adult Pilgrim figurines hold fall's abundance in their arms—pumpkins, apples, and more—while they sing out their thanks and praise. The adults were joined in 1997 by two Pilgrim children. Dressed in traditional Pilgrim dress of gray, black, and brown cottons, with their cornucopia of blessings from the earth, the four make a joyful fall decoration for any home.

Thankful for their survival in the new world, the Pilgrim settlers held a feast of thanksgiving. Joined by nearly one hundred of their Native American neighbors, the three-day event celebrated the friendship and unity between the two groups. One settler of Plymouth Colony, Edward Winslow, left a detailed account of the first Thanksgiving:

"Our harvest being gotten in, our governor sent four men on fowling, that so we might, after a special manner, rejoice together after we had gathered the fruit of our labors. We have found the Indians very faithful in their covenant of peace with us, very loving and

PILGRIM ADULTS (1996–) and PILGRIM CHILDREN (1997–)

ready to pleasure us. We often go to them and they come to us." Thanksgiving is a special time at Byers' Choice as a group of community-minded employees assemble complete Thanksgiving dinners for over two hundred of their neighbors in need.

One of the most popular Valentine myths holds that Valentine was in love with the daughter of his jailer and sent her a love letter signed, "With love from Valentine." Other tales have found their way down through the ages, evolving and becoming part of the Valentine's Day rituals that we know and celebrate today. In France, both sexes sometimes drew names from a "Valentine Box" used as a matchmaking system; hearts and flowers were used as love charms to bring about marriage. And in the early 1700s, a Valentine card custom began with English Valentine "writers." These writers were booklets of verse and messages to be copied and sent out. In the United States today, Valentine's Day is second only to Christmas in the number of greeting cards sent. The early 1980s saw the Byers foray into Spring Caroler figurines. The Valentine's Day and Easter children were identical except for their holiday accessories.

VALENTINE GIRL and BOY (1982–83)

Another holiday celebrated by Joyce with the creation of a figurine is St. Patrick's Day. The earliest observance of this holiday was in 1737 in Boston. It is named for St. Patrick, the patron saint of Ireland, who was born sometime in the latter part of the fourth

EASTER CHILDREN (1982–83)

century. In Ireland, this day is a religious holiday. Some say that St. Patrick taught his countrymen the art of distillation, which is why there is a lot of drinking involved with the day's celebrations. Other stories attributed to him are that he was a missionary who taught about the Trinity by using a shamrock. The first Byers' Choice Leprechauns, numbering 75, were custom made for Long's Jewelers in Boston.

The first observance of Mother's Day was on May 10, 1908, when Anna M. Jarvis, who adored her mother, and who worried that adult children neglected their mothers, lobbied to create an official day for mothers everywhere. Her efforts were rewarded with a resolution being passed in Congress in 1913. President Woodrow Wilson took it upon himself to officially request that the second Sunday in May be ordained for the observance of this holiday.

The Byers' first Mother's Day pieces were designed in 1987, especially for Bob and Joyce's mothers. They were so well liked by the employees of Byers' Choice that one hundred were made and test marketed, becoming the prototype of those produced the following year.

LEPRECHAUN (1982)

113

MOTHER'S DAY WITH DAUGHTER (1988)

MOTHER'S DAY WITH CARRIAGE (1989)

Joyce Remembers

Christmas in July! A friend and I introduced the wonderful customs of a true Pennsylvania Dutch Christmas to thousands of people who visited summer folk festivals in the mid 1970s.

In a corner of a large tent, we placed a wood stove in which we baked gingerbread boys, rosettes, and Whoopee Pies. The gingerbread smelled wonderful and put everyone into the Christmas spirit. The rosettes were also festive, but the favorites were the Whoopee Pies. The story behind this old Pennsylvania Dutch treat goes that when baking chocolate cakes, a mother would pour several large spoonfuls of batter onto a cookie sheet and bake them as cookies. When cooled, she sandwiched two together with vanilla icing. The kids, seeing the treats upon returning from school, would scream, "Whoopee!" thus, the name, Whoopee Pies.

The Christmas tree—cedar or juniper trees that could be found easily in the local fields—stood in another corner of the tent. It was decorated in the manner of the early 1800s with help from our children, who also helped us make all the ornaments. We used pretzels for good luck, strings of popcorn, ginger cookies decorated with colored icings and sugars, <u>schnitz</u> (circles of dried apple), nuts, beeswax tapers, and small toys and gifts. We made the ornaments so folk festival visitors could take a little bit of our old-fashioned Christmas home with them. One of my favorite decorations was a sheep re-created from descriptions in old

Moravian writings. Real wool covered the sheep's clay body and matchsticks were used for legs.

Our boys—dressed in calico shirts and straw hats—demonstrated how to make cookie ornaments from salt dough. <u>Distelfinks</u> (good luck birds) and pretzels were the most popular designs. On the weekends, our husbands would join us at the festival to help sell cookies and lemon sticks, another Pennsylvania Dutch treat. Children would break the end from a candy cane, cut a small hole in the top of a lemon or orange, and insert the stick into the fruit. The soft sugar center of the stick would dissolve as the acidic juice was sucked through it, flavoring the juice with sweet peppermint.

Although our Christmas in July didn't include a candlelit church service, new fallen snow, or colorful packages under the tree, the most important elements were there: family, friends, and sharing the spirit of the season with others.

Conclusion

Shout for joy to the Lord, all the earth.
Worship the Lord with gladness; come before him with joyful songs.
Know that the Lord is God.
It is he who made us, and we are his; we are his people, the sheep of his pasture.
Enter his gates with thanksgiving and his courts with praise;
give thanks to him and praise his name.
For the Lord is good and his love endures forever;
his faithfulness continues through all generations.
—Psalm 100: 1–5

Since Byers' Choice Ltd. has become so successful, it may be difficult to remember the days before the singing figurines found their market niche. In the mid 1970s, the Byers withstood several setbacks as they tried to figure out just what business would work for them. Characteristically, Bob believes those setbacks were all part of God's plan to steer the couple in a different direction.

"Setbacks build character and strength for the things God wants you to do later on," says Bob. "It's critical to realize and remember that God is in control. He's promised not to burden us with anything we can't carry. Focus on him and he can make anything happen. Look to God for solutions."

Hard work, creativity, and a Christian-based business attitude have come far in creating the success enjoyed by Byers' Choice, but there is still something mystical about it. Even for the serious collectors, the Byers' Choice Carolers are an emotional phenomenon, one which they can't fully explain.

"There is an emotional tugging at heartstrings brought out by the Carolers," muses Bob Emory, the Southeastern sales rep. "They're more than just a commodity sitting on a shelf. People relate to them somehow, and what Bob

Left to right: FRENCH HORN PLAYER (1992)

CLARINET PLAYER (1989)

ACCORDION PLAYER (1991)

VIOLIN PLAYER (1983–84)

MANDOLIN PLAYER (1990)

and Joyce want from people is for them to enjoy Christmas and enjoy what they've bought. It's not just a monetary thing; it's the genuine caring the Byers show.... Anyone involved with it has to have an open heart and be a giving person. It's not just a business."

The story of the Byers' Choice Christmas Carolers is a dream come true. With the blessings of God, and a lot of hard work, creativity, and imagination, Bob and Joyce Byers have seen their hobby grow into a successful family business dedicated to serving the customer and their employees, and also serving God and their community through their philanthropy. With the boundless energy of the Byers' Choice family, the Carolers should only get better.

WOMAN SELLING WREATHS (1997–)

TWENTIETH ANNIVERSARY SANTA IN SLEIGH (1998)

Appendix

CARING FOR YOUR CAROLERS

Softly apply some powder blush with a cotton swab to the cheeks of your Caroler if they begin to fade. Lips can be brushed with a natural shade of nail polish to bring back their original luster, and small chips on the base can be smoothed with a nail file and colored in with a felt-tip marker. Scuffed shoes can be fixed with black magic marker.

If your figurine's hair becomes too frizzy, spray lightly with a little hair spray. If her skirt

A collection of Carolers at Christmastime.

122

GARDENER (1997–)

WOMAN WITH GINGERBREAD HOUSE (1997–)

gets wrinkled or his jacket gets mussed while packed away, use a hand-held clothes steamer to ease out the wrinkles. A lint brush or the small attachment for the vacuum cleaner can help to remove loose fur or dust from clothes. To dust the face or base, try a small cosmetic brush and clean gently.

STORING YOUR CAROLERS

Avoid damp areas when storing your Carolers. High humidity can cause metal parts to rust or can increase mold on some fabrics. Blot away any excess water if your Caroler should happen to get wet, and dry with a blow dryer on the lowest setting.

It's a good idea to keep your Carolers safely stored well out of reach of any inquisitive pets. Cats and dogs have been known to be attracted to some of the materials in the Carolers and to chew them up.

Mice are also attracted to the Carolers, and find that their tissue paper bodies make great material for nest building. If you wrap your Carolers in tissue paper, adding a few moth-balls to the packing box, you will keep these rodents away. Avoid storing your Carolers in cedar, as the wood has been known to dissolve the paint on Carolers' faces. Finally, avoid dis-

playing them in bright sunlight. Prolonged exposure will fade the clothing and face paint.

It's important to store the Caroler figurines in a standing position. The house boxes, specially designed for the figurines, are perfect for this, as are boxes with partitions, which keep Carolers from bumping into one another. Crushed paper can be placed under skirts to help them hold their shape, but wrapping them in paper may crush the fabric. If a hat brim gets crushed, carefully manipulate the felt, or gently iron.

DISPLAYING YOUR CAROLERS

A trick to bring Carolers to life is to bend them into realistic positions. The only sensitive areas are where the head and feet are attached. Otherwise, the bodies have been designed to be fully bendable.

Some ideas for displaying your Carolers include: attaching Carolers to garlands atop doorways; clustering them on mantels with greenery, pinecones, and ribbon; or nestling a few of them into evergreen swags or wreaths.

For those with larger collections, Carolers can be easily attached to Christmas trees. You can decorate the tree using just the Carolers, or

SANTA IN GOLD SLEIGH (1998)

drape ribbons, garland, and bows to help embell-ish the display. Artificial trees and wreaths work well because you can use the wired branches to wrap around and hold the Carolers in place. If you put a candle in your window at Christmas, adding a Caroler and some greenery can make a warm and wonderful window display.

Another idea is to use the Carolers as the focal point of holiday centerpieces. Place a wreath in the center of the table and position the Carolers in the middle of the wreath, keeping in mind that they should relate to each other or "tell a story." You can spray artificial snow on the wreath and weave velvet ribbon throughout the arrangement. Remember, as a centerpiece it will be viewed from all sides, so place the Carolers so that everyone can see them.

For those who might like to incorporate a family heirloom, you can use platters, plates, bowls, or candleholders to enhance your display, as they can act as a base for your Carolers. A few branches of evergreens and holly placed around the figures and tied with flowing red velvet ribbons that cascade onto the table is sure to help create that wonderful Christmas spirit.

Keep in mind that the displays will be more successful if you use an odd number of Carolers, vary the height of the figures, and try to contrast the color and texture of their cloth-ing as much as possible. An accessory like the picket fence or lamppost placed in the right place with a few Carolers can add a warmth and charm to any area.

Index